While every precaution has been taken in the preparation of this book, the publisher assumes no responsibility for errors or omissions, or for damages resulting from the use of the information contained herein.

MALIGNANT NARCISSISM: UNDERSTANDING AND OVERCOMING MALIGNANT NARCISSISTIC ABUSE

First edition. July 1, 2019.

Copyright © 2019 Lauren Kozlowski.

ISBN: 978-1393922162

Written by Lauren Kozlowski.

GW00746101

Table of Contents

Malignant Narcissism: Understanding and Overcoming Malignant Narcissistic Abuse 1

Introduction 5

Chapter One - Explaining Malignant Narcissism and Recognizing a Malignant Narcissist 12

Chapter Two - Translating The Language of a Malignant Narcissist 25

Chapter Three - Lorna's Story: I Pity You, Abuser 34

Chapter Four - Can a Malignant Narcissist Ever Change? 38

Chapter Five - Anna's Story: I Feel Helpless 43

Chapter Six - The Dangers of a Malignant Narcissist: The Effects of Malignant Abuse 46

Chapter Seven - Clare's Story: It's Your Loss 54

Chapter Eight - The 'Perfect' Traits of the Prey of Malignant Narcissists 59

Chapter Nine - Trauma Bonded to Your Abuser 68

Chapter Ten - Escaping the Narcissist 76

Malignant Narcissism: Understanding and Overcoming Malignant Narcissistic Abuse

By Lauren Kozlowski

Before you dedicate your time to reading this book, here are a few questions you may need answering before you commit to reading it:

What is malignant narcissism?

This book goes into greater detail about malignant narcissism, but here is a condensed synopsis:

Malignant narcissism as a syndrome characterized by a narcissistic personality disorder, antisocial features, paranoid traits, and ego-syntonic aggression. Symptoms may include an absence of conscience, a psychological need for power, and a heightened sense of importance.

How is malignant narcissism different from narcissism?

The main difference between narcissism and malignant narcissism is that malignant narcissism includes features of other personality disorders, therefore it consists of a broader range of symptoms than pathological narcissism (or sometimes just referred to NPD) alone.

With malignant narcissism, the NPD is accompanied by additional symptoms of antisocial, paranoid and sadistic personality disorders. Whilst a person with NPD will purposefully damage others in pursuit of their own desires, they may come to regret their actions and will, in some circumstances, show remorse. Because antisocial personality disorder traits are exhibited in malignant narcissism, the malignant narcissist has a noticeable lack of empathy compared to someone with NPD alone and will lack feelings of guilt or remorse for the damage they cause.

Since sadism is often considered a feature of malignant narcissism, an individual with the syndrome can not only lack feelings of guilt or remorse for hurting others but often derives pleasure from the gratuitous infliction of mental or physical pain on others.

Are you a psychologist/therapist?

I'm not. I'm a former victim of a malignant narcissist, and I was brought up by a violent, narcissistic father who I now believe to be a malignant narc. My abusive relationship lasted seven years, and the aftermath of my leaving also resulted in my narcissistic ex becoming violent, stalking me and using his 'flying monkeys' to help aid him in his reign of abuse over me. This made the time I was trapped in the cycle of abuse much longer than the seven years I spent with him.

Therefore, this book is not meant to be a mental health guide, or offer you professional advice. Instead, I want to offer you my experience and knowledge of the topic, as well as being a tool for you to refer to if you're in (or were in) a relationship with a malignant narcissist. This is my recollection of events, which means I don't recite hypothetical scenarios from a textbook or use psychoanalytic lingo - I tell you my story and how I overcome the abuse of a malignant narcissist and offer you my thoughts and opinion on the disorder.

My credentials for writing this book is an upbringing with a psychotic narcissist and a long term relationship with a malignant narcissist. I've seen a therapist, which did help me overcome some of the trauma, but the real healing began when I reached out to other victims of abuse. Being able to talk freely and knowing they understood and fully empathized with my situation really allowed me to feel like I wasn't alone. Listening to other people recount their stories and how the abuse affected them also helped me gain a broader understanding of narcissism, as well as often finding that their stories overlapped with my own. We all had similar stories to tell.

The things you'll read in this book are things I learned during my relationship, as well as after the relationship had ended when I devoted myself to researching narcissism. There are also things I learned from counseling, therapists and other survivors scattered throughout this book, too.

What will you cover in this book?

I begin by explaining who I am and giving you a little more context about my situation in an abusive relationship. I will go on to explain my understanding of malignant narcissism, and how you can recognize a malignant narc. I'll outline the dangers of being involved with a malignant, as well as offering you my findings of what makes the 'perfect' victim for a narcissist. I also go on to discuss leaving an abusive narcissist, as well as the dangers associated with his and how to navigate this dangerous territory safely. I discuss trauma bonding, and how this can often tie us to the abusive relationship. Finally, I have a chapter dedicated to healing from the trauma and abuse associated with being in a relationship with a malignant narcissist.

*

Hopefully, I've answered any questions you may have, and you're now certain that this is the book for you. If so, I thank you for reading and I'm glad you chose this book! I hope it offers you some hope, guidance, and knowledge, as well as a comforting sense of familiarity - a sense that someone has been through what you're going through, but has come out of the other side.

Here's to healing.

Introduction

It's hard to explain how I got caught in the net of narcissism. My ex, a malevolent, malignant narcissist, snared me in his web of abuse and I couldn't find a way out for such a long time. It's hard to explain this to most people, because I'm met with frustrating responses like, "why didn't you *just leave* him?", or "why didn't you just tell your parents what was going on?"

If you're reading this book, I'm going to assume that you know as well as I do - simply 'just leaving' a narcissist isn't as easy as people try to make out, let alone someone as evil as a malignant narcissist.

What people don't understand is that abusers don't unmask themselves as evil, vicious and spiteful from the get-go. Abusers, just like mine, will shower you with attention and affection in the beginning. They'll make you feel special. They'll charm their way into your affection and be committed to earning your trust. They'll appear to you, and everyone else around you, as perfect.

When I began dating my abusive ex, I felt like I was on cloud nine. I'd wonder how I got so lucky. Things were moving fast with him, but I wasn't worried - he had rapidly gained my trust and I was fine with how quickly our relationship had developed. Within a few months, he'd told me he loved me and we'd moved in together.

My little bubble of happiness soon burst, though. My ex would have terrible mood swings. He'd dangle his love for me over my head, using my adoration for him as a way to manipulate me into doing things he wanted me to do. He would become enraged with me at the slightest thing, calling me all the names under the sun for offenses I'd apparently committed against him.

Whilst he was always somewhat possessive over me, this got a lot worse. When we started dating, his slight possessiveness was something I'd mistaken for protectiveness. I thought he was protecting me from 'bad' friends, or men who had 'bad intentions' for me. It was comforting and endearing that he was looking after me and my feelings. However, it soon transpired that his overprotectiveness was instead sheer possessiveness, and he starting ramping this up by accusing me of being a cheat and telling me I was untrustworthy. He also questioned where I was spending my money, and would check my bus ticket when I got home from work to check what time I got on the bus home. The bus journey home took around twenty minutes, and if the time stamp on the bus ticket was over this time limit, he would accuse me of all kinds of things that I would be 'doing behind his back' in those extra minutes.

The bad treatment was ramped up even further around the fifth month of the relationship. The cruel treatment didn't just happen overnight; it was a gradual thing. And the cruel, humiliating treatment was also mixed with glimmers of the man I fell in love with, as he would also tell me he loved me and how much he wanted a great future with me. This confused me, as when he was cruel to me, he was *really cruel,* but his words of commitment to me would make me believe that it was me who instigated the cruelty he'd bestow on me. He said he wanted to be with me, but I believed it was my actions who drove him to treat me the way he did, so I endured it with this in mind.

As I mentioned, around the fifth month was the month he stepped his narcissism up a notch. Humiliating me in front of his friends became something he took great joy in. Telling me how attractive other women found him and how he could easily meet someone else was something he was keen to remind me of. He would lie to me profusely, and even if I knew he was lying, he would point blank swear on my life he was telling the truth. His aggression became something that didn't just intimidate me anymore - it downright terrified me. He could be laughing and smiling, and if I said something he deemed 'wrong', the smile would easily revert to a menacing scowl, and he'd berate me with gritted teeth, spitting as he hissed vile words at me. It was scary. Even if it was in front of other people or if we had guests, he didn't care - he would humiliate me then talk to our awkward guests as if nothing had happened.

Not only did his menacing behavior scare me, I started to become aware that he didn't have a 'limit' or an 'off switch' like most people. He would go that step too far, and once he got there, he could go further, if he wanted. He would say hurtful things about me, really personal things that he knew would hurt me badly. He'd use personal things I'd told him and use them against me, threatening to tell other people about it if he decided one day he wanted to. He would hang that over my head.

He also had a very large appetite for admiration. Not just from me, but from other women too. Of course, he made me well aware of how many women fawned over him, and he'd even flirt with other women in front of me. If I dared confront him about this, he would explode with rage. He'd say I was a psycho bitch, full of insecurity and jealousy.

'If I *was* flirting, how can you blame me, when you're such a psycho?', is as close to admitting he was in the wrong as I would ever get.

So much for the funny, witty, caring and charming man I thought he was. The pre-commitment phase is the time the narcissist utilizes to snare their victim. Their 'good guy' mask is firmly on, not slipping until they have their victim's love, trust, and admiration. However, reality soon sets in. It took five months in my case; it can happen much sooner or later, but one thing is for sure, reality does set in. The mask does slip. Slowly but surely, it slips bit by bit, revealing the malignant narcissist piece by piece, until you're engulfed by the disturbing reality of the relationship you're in.

I bit the bait and fell hook, line, and sinker. I'm not someone who you'd describe as gullible, vulnerable or meek - I'm not 'narcissist' fodder or someone who you'd picture as easy prey for a malignant narcissist. I'll discuss the traits that a malignant narcissist looks for in their victims later on, and it's not the inexperienced, shy, love-seeking person that a lot of people think. I am worldly-wise, intelligent and keen to achieve, and never in a million years did I think I'd be snared into an abusive relationship, much less stay in one.

But for seven years, that's what I did.

For seven years I feared for my safety. I was stripped of my confidence. I was inaccurately portrayed to other people as a cheater, liar or psychopath. My upset and pain became a source of joy and pleasure to the person in my life who ought to love me. I was scared of saying the 'wrong' thing that would enrage my volatile ex. I was treated with suspicion, disdain and a lack of empathy. I was in purgatory, unable to find a reason why I was there or a way to get myself out of it.

Growing up (although I didn't realize this at the time), my father also showed a lot of signs that pointed toward him being a malignant narcissist.

He struck fear into our family, playing the loving, doting dad only when it benefited him. I only began to understand what my dad was when I grew up and fell straight into a relationship with someone who mirrored him so accurately.

When I was a child, coming home from school was something I absolutely dreaded because of my father. I didn't know what I was going to come home to. Would my father be in a rage, and if so, how would my presence make that worse? Would he have trashed the house? Would he have invited his friends around, who would proceed to run amok in our house? Would my father be arguing with my mother?

The last one would be the outcome I dreaded the most; I would hate when my father would set himself upon my mother. In his paranoid state, he would often accuse her of cheating, plotting to kill him, stealing from him, or some other wild accusation would be flung her way. This often leads to violence. Even in his wobbly, drunken states, my father would easily overpower my mother.

These paranoia-induced beatings would be something I would bear witness to throughout my childhood. No amount of screaming or pleading from me would stop my father when he got something irrational in his head.

When I was very young I was a daddy's girl, wanting to spend all my time with him and just be in his company. As I grew older, his narcissism got much worse. He would scream at us, shouting obscenities, play his music unbearably loud until the early hours of the morning and seemed to take great pleasure in witnessing how distressed this made us. Getting up for school was so hard when I'd been up all night because of my dad's loud ruckus.

He would often pick fights with the neighbors, sometimes even knocking on their doors in his underwear in order to provoke a reaction from them. Some of our neighbors were elderly, and it broke my heart that my dad would disrupt them in this embarrassing, antisocial way. I didn't want the neighbors to think ill of me, and I would feel ashamed every time I saw them in the street after my dad had been banging on their door at three in the morning. They were clearly scared of him, but there was nothing I could do: I was just a child.

He would also humiliate me in front of my peers and friends. I was too ashamed to have friends sleepover or come for dinner as they would see my dad's behavior. From him falling over drunk, saying inappropriate things to my friends or screaming accusations at my mum, these were the things that my school mates would have to witness if they were staying over. Of course, once my friends found out about my 'mental' father, it became something they would use to make fun of me. They would goad me about his embarrassing behavior, tell the other children what my home life was like and mock me about my father's aggression toward my mother.

To someone who hasn't been through this, they would argue that being brought up by someone so viciously narcissistic and cruel would deter me from ever entering a relationship with someone similar. Of course, this would be the case in an ideal world, but unfortunately, it's a common misconception that

I'll explain more about my relationship throughout this book, and use it to help guide you towards understanding malignant narcissism, knowing the dangers associated with it, and how to protect yourself from it moving forward. Being in a relationship with a malignant narcissist means your confidence has been ground down so far that you question your own logic, and you're unsure of your own decision making. This means fighting back and clawing yourself out of purgatory is almost unthinkable; the odds seem so stacked up against you, how could you ever try to conquer them and break free?

I know you can. Because I did. And I want to share my story, helping you understand this contemptuous and complex form of abuse and ultimately, which allows you to break free from it.

Chapter One - Explaining Malignant Narcissism and Recognizing a Malignant Narcissist

The term malignant narcissist is used to describe a personality disorder that's on the more 'extreme' or 'dangerous' side of the narcissistic spectrum. A malignant narcissist mixes parts of other personality disorders, resulting in this amalgamated, extreme and aggressive personality disorder.

One of the main characteristics, or traits, of a narcissist, is their belief of superiority and their prevalent grandiose behavior. This results in their persistent need for admiration in order to feed their narcissistic supply. Narcissists are also known for their deficiency in empathy, and lack of sensitivity towards others, although malignant narcissists don't even try to feign feelings of empathy, like other types of narcissist would.

Malignant narcissism, however, goes a bit further than that. This personality disorder includes traits of paranoia, antisocial personality disorder and also ego-syntonic aggression (which, in a nutshell, is a way to describe someone whose behaviors match the goals of their ego. Their actions run parallel to their ideal self-image).

It's important to note here that the term 'malignant narcissist' isn't a diagnostic term. Otto Kernberg first used the term 'malignant narcissism' in psychology in 1984, so this term is a relatively new one when it comes to disorders like this. Otto is known for his psychoanalytic theories on borderline personality and narcissistic pathology, and he is one of the few psychologists to delve into this topic and shed some light on the disorder.

Otto summarised malignant narcissism as a severe personality disorder that was identifiable by its antisocial behavior, ego-syntonic sadism, and paranoid orientation. If you were ever wondering what the main difference between a narcissist and a malignant narcissist is, it's that narcissism is a diagnostic term. Whilst the term 'malignant' was coined by a psychoanalyst, it's not recognized as a diagnosable form of narcissism.

Malignant narcissism is on the severe end of the narcissistic spectrum and has the potential to ruin lives with its sadistic, emotionally crippling and tornado-like force. The toxic, aggressive and chaotic behavior of a malignant narcissist makes them someone potentially very dangerous to have in your life. Their complete lack of true self-awareness makes them devoid of any capacity to want to change, which allows them to continue their destructive, harmful and threatening behavior.

If you're unsure as to whether or not you have a malignant narcissist in your life, here are some signs that will help you determine your answer. You don't need to see each and every one of these signs in someone else to decide whether or not they are a malignant narcissist, but rather you will likely see at least a few of these signs in someone who is malignant:

Self-enhancement

Self-enhancement is a prominent aspect of a narcissistic personality, although arguably much more so in someone who is a malignant narcissist. A malignant narcissist will view themselves in a highly positive and superior light in comparison to other people. They have this unwavering belief that they are special, unique and above other people.

People with a high level of narcissism, like malignant narcissists, tend to exaggerate and overestimate their abilities, skills, looks or any other braggable trait or characteristic they think they have. Malignant narcissists, fuelled by their lust for power, believe they are better than other people. This is still the case even if they are presented with evidence to support the contrary, such as exam results or an IQ test. This reality of the narcissist not being as great as they believe would be met with defensiveness and would be challenged by the narcissist. A malignant narcissist often cannot accept the truth, and will often try and attack it with defensiveness, verbal abuse or degradation.

For example, if you mentioned something that the malignant may have failed, such as a test, they won't take responsibility for that. They may say things like, 'the test was stupid - it holds no merit', 'the examiner didn't know what he was doing' or 'it was rigged'.

Malignants don't let irrefutable evidence get in the way of their inflated self-assessment.

My ex was the bee's knees according to him, and was too good for many things in his life (his job, his social circle, *me*), and didn't hesitate in letting me know this.

Sadism

A malignant narcissist is wired to deliberately cause suffering, stress, harm and upset in order to feed their narcissistic ego. A word to summarise the hurtful and torturous behaviors of a malignant narcissist is sadism. A sadist gets enjoyment and pleasure from the suffering and humiliation of others. Just like a sadist, a malignant will purposefully inflict emotional, verbal and even physical abuse on their victim to satisfy their own cruel, twisted needs.

This very deliberate treatment is dished out without mercy or guilt, and the malignant will feel gratification from the pain that they inflict on their victim.

For example, my ex loved to torture me about traumatic things that had happened to me in the past or force me into talking about things I felt really uncomfortable or upset about. He told me that my father didn't love me and that, when I was a child, my mother worked long hours so she didn't have to be around me. My ex would tell me I was a burden as a child, and still a burden as an adult. When he asked me if I felt any guilt about this, I plucked up the courage to say 'no' - this, of course, only fuelled his rage, and he berated me for my 'blatant arrogance'. He would use things against me, twist what I said and make up things that I'd supposedly told him, all to fuel his own sadism - he loved to make me feel utter devastation. It seemed like the ultimate pleasure for him.

Manipulation

To be more specific, a malignant will be very proactive in the manipulation of their victim. Whilst all narcissists are prone to being highly manipulative, a malignant narcissist will be especially motivated when it comes to exercising control over their victim.

Typically, a narcissist will see an opportunity to manipulate and take it. They'll take advantage of someone's vulnerability without a second thought and be opportunistic when it comes to exercising control over their victim.

However, a malignant narcissist is much more proactive in their manipulative behavior. Instead of waiting around for an opportunity to manipulate, a malignant will be much more forceful with their manipulative tactics. They are proactive in their execution of manipulation. They don't hang around, waiting for the perfect time to manipulate - when a malignant wants power and control, irrespective of the situation, they'll manipulate without hesitation.

As I mentioned before, malignant narcissists get enjoyment from making others suffer, and manipulation is a key part of that enjoyment. Whilst manipulation, for a narcissist, is primarily a way to gain control over their victim, there is also a secondary aspect to it that the narcissist derives pleasure from: the hurt, confusion and suffering it causes for their victim.

A malignant narcissist's manipulation is dangerously calculated, and it's something they've had plenty of practice in over the years. The end goal for the effort they put into manipulating their victim is for the victim to feel so helpless and stripped of their free will that they're unable to remove themselves from their situation. This gives the malignant complete control - precisely what they crave.

Antisocial Behavior

A malignant exhibits some of the same behaviors as someone who has been diagnosed with an antisocial personality disorder, and there are quite a lot of cross-overs between the two disorders. Much like someone with an antisocial personality, a malignant is prone to hostility, aggression, unprovoked moods and volatility.

They're often pathological liars who don't have morals when it comes to cheating or lying, which only adds to the dangers they present to their victims. A malignant will often be willing to fight or show aggression at any time, ensuring the victim is kept on their toes and unable to predict the toxic behavior that's inflicted upon them.

Inability to accept criticism

If you dare to point out a malignants flaws or offer some constructive criticism, you'd be doing this at your own peril - they are dangerously hypersensitive to criticism.

Anything that affronts a malignant narcissist's sense of their 'perfect' self would be deemed as an attack towards them and would be responded to with an aggressive defense. Taking feedback on board and understanding someone else's point of view isn't something a malignant narcissist will consider doing: their go-to response to anything critical is to attack.

The malignant has such a fragile sense of self underneath their intimidating and domineering front.

Paranoia

Malignant narcissists don't trust. They are always suspicious, even if they have no real or apparent reason to be, and have an unwavering belief that others are out to get them. Even if they don't outright say that they think everyone is against them, their actions and behaviors can often show this; they'll never give too much away, and see most people as a threat. People are simply there to be manipulated, or so the narcissist thinks - they won't let themselves ever be on the receiving end of such treatment.

This probably goes a long way in explaining why the malignant narcissist is so paranoid. They seek to use, abuse and manipulate others for their own sadistic gain so they believe others are out to do the same. The malignant narcissist is hyper-vigilant because they believe others have the same capacity of cruel, abusive and aggressive behavior as they do, and because of this, view people as threats.

This, in turn, leads the malignant narc to become obsessed with what other people (namely their victim) are doing. They will try to control the movements and actions of their victims to ensure they do and day as the narc wants, thus helping to contain the risk of being played at their own sadistic game.

Lack of Empathy

All narcissists lack empathy - it's a key characteristic that's become synonymous with the personality disorder. However, there are varying degrees to this. Some narcissists, on the milder end of the spectrum, can express some empathy - not in the same way as a person who didn't have NPD, but they're still able to exhibit *some* empathetic behaviors and actions. Even so, feeling flutters of empathy may not be enough to change the way a narcissist behaves, but they may be able to understand remorse or regretful feelings. This is a far cry to what's on the other end of the spectrum - a malignant narcissist. A malignant narcissist absolutely lacks empathy.

They can't feel empathy. To put themselves in someone else's shoes and try to understand their feelings is beyond alien to them. Even the *want* to try and do that isn't there - they don't *want* to relate to other people in that way. It isn't something the malignant finds beneficial. Feeling guilt and remorse for the pain and suffering they cause isn't something the narcissist can comprehend - their empathy tank is completely depleted.

Inability to Accept Responsibility For Their Actions

This could be a trait that's used to describe quite a lot of people in your life - friends, family, co-workers, and ex-partners. At some point in life, we've all had a hard time accepting full responsibility for the way we've behaved or made someone else feel. We're only human after all, and sometimes the only reaction we can muster to a perceived attack is to be defensive.

However, a malignant narcissist, as with most things they do, will take this to a whole new level.

They'll twist and warp the truth to make it seem as if their vile words or actions are justified. They'll push the blame onto the victims, externalizing blame wherever they can, making sure the finger is never pointed at them. They'll gaslight and manipulate to deflect any responsibility for their actions, even in the face of irrefutable evidence, where it's almost laughable that the narc feels like it's acceptable to lie. It's almost as if their chutzpah makes their lies all the more believable, even though deep down, the victim knows they're being lied to.

Attention Seeking Behavior

'Attention seeking behavior' can also be translated to: *ways to obtain narcissistic supply.*

As you know, a narcissist is nothing without their supply, and they often get this with their frequent seeking of adoration, attention, and affection from others. This tops up their supply. For someone who has moderate narcissism, or someone who simply just exhibits some slight narcissistic traits, positive reinforcement of their attention seeking behavior will boost their self-worth. It'll satisfy their need to feed on other people's emotions.

However, with a malignant narcissist, it's the negative attention that really gets them going. They're not fearful of confrontation, so playing the 'bad guy' and soaking up all the negative emotions that come from that can really satisfy a malignant narcissist. Not much is off bounds for the malignant when it comes to courting negative attention - they'll attack physically, morally and verbally.

Envious

The malignant narcissist holds themselves in very high regard, and have a need to be better than everyone else around them. If they happen to come across someone who they deem to be 'better' than them, or who trumps them in any way, then the narc is riddled with envy. This can happen when they encounter someone who's better off financially than they are, someone who has a better car or lifestyle, or someone who has skills the narcissist would like to have; the narc hates to see other people having the things they want.

You've likely witnessed this envious behavior for yourself. If the narcissist is confronted with someone who has the things they want, they'll find it hard to keep their envy from externalizing - they'll put that person down, belittle them and make them feel as if they aren't deserving of the good things they own or do. The malignant has great difficulty in disguising their bitterness towards those who have more than they do, although I'm not sure if they ever really make a genuine effort to hide their sour feelings in this situation.

Should they have the chance, the malignant will sabotage (or attempt to sabotage) the success of someone they're envious of. They might start a smear campaign against that person in order to blacken their reputation, or they'll offer them bad advice on purpose to steer them down a wicked path of failure.

A malignant narcissist enjoys basking in the failure of other people, and they'll revel in the pain and suffering this can cause.

Not all malignant narcissists will do this outwardly, some will choose to keep their glee internalized so they can appear to outsiders to have the human emotions of empathy and sympathy. However, a lot of malignant narcs don't care too much about this, and will externally show their enjoyment at someone else's failings.

Charming

After all, we didn't fall for the monster we discovered we'd ended up with, did we? We fell for the charming, love-bombing, ideal person they made out they were. They charmed their way into our heart, as a malignant narcissist is so good at doing. The charm can be flicked on like a switch, depending on who they're with and the situation, and it can be turned off just as quick.

When you first meet a malignant narc, they're likely to be the friendly, helpful, funny and kind person you thought they were - they're well rehearsed in their charm offensive, and it's worked on other people who came before you (these are likely the same people who the narc tells you 'wronged' them or took advantage of them.)

Charm is how the narcissist will reel their victim in. It's the mask they wear to cover their true identity of toxicity, manipulation, cruelty, and control. The narc is so well versed in their charm offensive that they can use it to make their victim act in a certain way or change their opinion of other people.

This false sincerity is almost undetectable, and the love-bombing that accompanies the charm cements the place the abuser has in our heart; this, of course, is when the mask usually slips. They don't need to pretend anymore.

Hopefully, the traits outlined in this chapter have helped you decide if you're dealing with a malignant narcissist. As I mentioned, they don't need to fit into each category, but chances are, they'll have most of the characteristics mentioned in this section.

It's important to remember that malignant narcissism is not an 'official' diagnosis, which means that it's open to interpretation. Some people that I've spoken to about it place it just under psychopathy, others think it's a disorder equal with psychopathy.

Keep in mind that all these terms – narcissist, psychopath, sociopath — are terms made up and used by mental health professionals to describe groups of people who have certain behaviors. Also, the illnesses associated with these terms aren't the type of illness you can see under a microscope (although it may be worth a mention here that brain scans have shown that those with narcissistic personality disorder appear to have less brain activity in areas related to empathy.)

People that lay on the 'dark spectrum' - those who are labeled psychotic, sociopathic and severely narcissistic - are not the sort to go to the doctor themselves and seek help for their disorder.

Often, they don't think they have anything is wrong with them, so going and speaking to a therapist about it is out of the question. They're very unlikely to show up to therapy of their own accord. This means that clinical evidence is limited when it comes to those who are on the 'dark' end of the spectrum.

With this in mind, I hope the above chapter has helped you as a tool to understand the type of person you're dealing with.

Chapter Two - Translating The Language of a Malignant Narcissist

A malignant narcissist is very deliberate with their choice of words. They use them to distort your perception of yourself, the relationship you have, and reality as a whole, in order to maintain that much-needed control over you. The language of a malignant narcissist serves to gaslight you, invalidate your emotions, devalue your character and drain you until you no longer have the will to put up a struggle. Think of their words as an elaborate magician's trick, complete with mirrors, smoke, and sleight of hand movements that are too quick for you to notice; their words are verbal trickery that they use for their own manipulative gains.

It was only after speaking to other former victims of malignant narcissism that I realized how the phrases or the 'narcissistic speak' from abusers is similar in each case; when each victim recounted the things their abuser would say to them it was like they were echoing the stories of other victims.

It also rang true for me - I was taken aback by how almost identical some of the language used by other abusers was to the phrased used by my own abuser. The group that I was speaking to about 'narcissists speak' helped me compile a list of commonly used phrases, and whilst the malignant narcissist in your life may not use each phrase word for word, I'm sure they'll have their own variation of the phrase that means the same thing. Here's what we came up with, and I've added a translation of what each commonly used narcissistic phrase really means:

Phrase #1 - 'You're crazy', 'you need mental help' or 'you have a mental health problem'.

What the narcissist is saying here is, 'you're getting too close to revealing what's behind my mask and are attempting to hold me accountable for my own actions - I'd rather make you think that **you're** the problem.'

The more the narcissist tells you that you're unhinged, that you need help or are deranged, the more inclined you are to believe that. And, once the narcissist has you considering that you could well have problems, then they're able to brush off the responsibility of their actions onto you.

It's a brutally manipulative way for the narcissist to ensure you don't attempt to make them accountable for their vile behavior, and by projecting their own deficiencies onto you, they maintain the upper hand in the relationship. By bringing your mental health into question, the malignant narc is also undermining you and bringing into dispute your credibility. What makes it all the more manipulative is when the abuser provokes reactions from their victim that aids in their 'crazy' diagnosis. When the abuser makes you feel so helplessly frustrated and distorted, you can often begin to exhibit behaviors that help the narcissist that their 'you need mental help' diagnosis is correct. This can also aid the abuser in convincing others that this is the case, too; they have 'proof' that you're unhinged by the way you're acting. Unbeknown to others, it's the abuser that's provoking and inducing your actions and reactions.

Phrase #2 - 'You're so jealous'.

This commonly used phrase among malignant narcissists can be translated as 'I want to make you feel unstable and insecure, and make you doubt your place in my heart - don't you dare question my flirting, affairs or inappropriate interactions with others or I'll make sure you know you're the problem'.

This phrase is yet another way for the narcissist to heap their own vile behavior onto you, to make you the problem, not them. Of course, the narcissist is aware deep down that they're the issue, but they won't be held responsible for it. To the narcissist, it's *your* problem that you can't retain your emotions whilst they openly flirt, galavant with others behind your back or demeaningly compare you to others - you should know your place and not bring it up. Otherwise, not only are you at risk of being dropped for the next thing that comes along, but you'll also be blamed for the abuser doing so.

Your jealousy is a hot commodity to the abuser. Malignant narcissists are known to utilize the adoration and apparent attraction of others to manipulate their victim. As they're known charmers, there's always a potential 'new' partner on the horizon - or so they're keen to make you think. The malignant narc wants you to believe that they're in high demand, and as such, you best treat them with the respect they command, or they can up and move on quicker than you can imagine.

A common theme among malignant narcissists is their use of 'triangulation'. This means the abuser is purposefully creating a strong sense of rivalry, jealousy, and competition within the gaggle of potential suitors they've created. This gives the warped narcissist a sense of power and control, as well as the ego boost they so desperately need.

Provoking their victim with blatant flirting or adultery, then calling them 'jealous' and painting them out to be crazy when they react is a fun game for the narcissist. Torturing their victims emotionally by calling them insecure, envious and controlling is a much-loved projection the narcissist likes to display when they've been caught cheating. Whilst it's a source of enjoyment for the narcissist, it's also a way to avoid taking responsibility and is a way to further make their victim wonder if they really are going crazy.

Phrase #3 - 'You can't take a joke'.

You can interpret this phrase as meaning: 'I'm thinly disguising my abusive words and actions as a joke. I want to reap the pleasure of putting you down and calling you nasty names, but I won't be held responsible for the pain that causes. That's your fault for not having a sense of humor'.

The old 'just a joke' deflection is a cruel, frustrating phrase to listen to when we try to explain to the abuser how their depraved words have made us feel. Not only have we had to endure the pain of being verbally abused, but the blame for that hurt and humiliation is heaped onto us as well for 'not having a sense of humor'.

Of course, you know when someone is just joking and when someone is maliciously putting you down and hiding behind it as simply being 'jesting'. However, the denial from the abuser of the intent behind their comments serves to make you feel like you're too sensitive or can't take banter. When a malignant narcissist doles out their 'jokes', they're cutting jibes, taunts about your insecurities, contemptuous comments, and name-calling - they're very clearly not witty gags, but rather they're verbal assaults.

The narcissist will evade the responsibility of this by blaming your inability to understand or appreciate their humor on your offense at their joke.

Phrase #4 - 'You're too sensitive'.

This one is quite simply translated as: 'You're not oversensitive, it's me that's *insensitive*'. In order to override any blame for their callous, hurtful and downright unempathetic actions, the malignant narcissist will blame the victim for being 'too sensitive'.

When the narcissist hurts and degrades, this provides them with the sick pleasure and stimulation they're after. The reactions you have to their abuse is a huge source of enjoyment for them.

By making you feel responsible for the hurt and anguish their comments and actions cause you, the narcissist is also planting seeds that the severity of their abuse is in your head - that you're an overreacting, emotionally oversensitive exaggerator, and that you're blowing things out of proportion.

You may or may not be a sensitive person, that fact is irrelevant. If your spouse hurts your feelings, they ought to allow you to feel those emotions and take on board your upset at their words or actions. This should help them shape their future behavior, so they don't make you feel that way moving forward. Instead, a malignant narcissist will intently still focus on your insecurities and 'sensitive' subjects in order to get the 'overly sensitive' reaction from you, which allows them (in their mind) to carry on with their vile behavior and blame you for it.

Phrase #5 - 'Why can't you move on and forget about it?'

Translated: 'I know you're still hurt and in pain over that abusive episode, but stop mentioning it. I want to move on and brush over it so I can continue to behave like I want without you constantly bringing the past up. To shut you up, I might lovebomb you; I'll make you think it won't happen again, just so you stop going on. Of course, that won't last - it's all part of my cycle of abuse'.

This is the classic abuse cycle in action; the hot-and-cold attitude of the abuser when they're confronted with abusive episodes of the past. These breadcrumbs of love lead you thinking that you'll get the 'old them' back - the person you fell for during the honeymoon phase of the relationship. In reality, the breadcrumbing is just another manipulation tactic to keep you in their grasp.

The 'why can't you just forget about it' phrase serves to help sustain the cycle of abuse, so you can magically forget about their horrific treatment of you to enable them to resume their abusive pattern. Of course, you're not going to get sudden amnesia and forget all about the torture and pain they've inflicted - but that doesn't faze the narcissist.

Phrase #6 - 'I never said that!'

This commonly used phrase among narcissists is to be interpreted as: 'I'm going to make you question and doubt yourself. I'll give you false memories that'll you'll accept as the truth. I'll make you wonder if you really are imagining things, which takes the heat off of you exposing my abuse for what it is'.

This is a classic gaslighting phrase that, simple as it is, is a very successful manipulation tool that malignant narcissists utilize to 'crazy make' their victim. When someone is so sure and insistent that they *never* said something, this eventually chips away at your recollection of events. When doubt creeps in, you begin to think *maybe* they didn't say that after all... perhaps you misunderstood or misheard.

This shows how powerful and effective continual denial is for a narcissistic abuser; it can make their victim really start to believe that they're really making things up or have a dangerous imagination.

Phrase #7 - 'I'm not the problem, you're the problem!'

This blameful phrase can be transcribed as: 'I won't have you know the truth that I'm the issue here. You'll take my vile treatment and verbal attacks and you'll accept my constant goalpost moving and expectations of you. I'll make up problems and issues I have with you, only to watch you try and fix these fabricated issues in vain. By making you the problem, I can continue to feel entitled to continue to treat you the way I do'.

This narcissistic phrase can be referred to as 'malignant projection' - making the victim believe that *they're* the narcissist who has abusive and malignant tendencies. This is a calculating and callous move by the narcissist, as it makes the victim rethink their reactions to the abuse inflicted upon them. By projecting, the narcissist makes the victim think that their reactions are the problem, not the actual vile behavior of the narcissist.

****

If you're in a relationship with a malignant narcissist, or ever had the displeasure of being involved with one, then the above phrases will resonate with you. You'll have heard them, or most of them at least, numerous times. And you very likely remember how they made you feel when you were subjected to them: frustrated, helpless, confused, anger with no way to express it, and sheer disorientation at your own perceptions.

Here's a quick recap of the phrases:

Phrase #1 - 'You're crazy', 'you need mental help' or 'you have a mental health problem'

Phrase #2 - 'You're so jealous'

Phrase #3 - 'You can't take a joke'

Phrase #4 - 'You're too sensitive'

Phrase #5 - 'Why can't you move on and forget about it?'

Phrase #6 - 'I never said that!'

Phrase #7 - 'I'm not the problem, you're the problem!'

Chapter Three - Lorna's Story: I Pity You, Abuser

Throughout the book, I want to give more insights, opinions, and stories from other victims of malignant narcissism. I want this book to be as comprehensive as possible when it comes to understanding malignant narcissism, and I feel it's important to include the thoughts and feelings of others who have been (or currently are) victim to narcissism.

I will begin with Lorna, who was in a relationship with a malignant narcissist for almost a decade. Lorna left her abuser two years ago but has only recently found the peace and closure she has been searching for. This is because her narcissistic ex was relentlessly contacting her, finding out her number even after she'd changed it, and was mercilessly hoovering her back up and dropping her as it suited him. Lorna was so trauma bonded to her ex that it took her a long time to finally let go, and since she has, she's been a valuable and inspiration member of the survivor community.

Here is Lorna's letter to her abusive ex that she wrote as part of her healing process. She didn't send this to her ex, but she used it as a form of therapy by externalizing her inner feelings and putting pen to paper (or fingers to keyboard, in this case):

Once upon a time, I would have done anything for you. I adored you-you were my world, and I did everything you ever asked of me, even if it meant I was left with nothing. The only thing I ever asked of you was to be nice to me, to be kind... just to respect me. That's the only thing I ever asked.

I lost all of my friends because you told me they were bad for me. I stopped going to the gym because you were paranoid I was meeting another man there. I avoided any social situation because I was scared of how you would react if you knew I was talking to other men, even though you must have known I'd never have been unfaithful. I missed my sister's 40th birthday because you didn't like her husband, and refused to go - and as much as you told me to go alone, I knew if I did, there would be hell to pay. I lost so much of me when I was with you.

I was constantly in a state of fear. The smallest thing would anger you or upset you, and you would always change the goalposts. You slowly and systematically eroded my self-worth; you told me I was an uneducated, dumb, 'simpleton' who wasn't destined to go far in life. Because of this, whilst I was with you, I avoided putting myself up for a promotion or pay raises at work. You told me I was 'funny looking', or joke about my looks, knowing how much it hurt me, yet you still wouldn't relent. You were 'joking', after all. You told me make-up didn't suit me, that I should accept I was a plain Jane and not bother 'dolling' myself up - there wasn't much to work with anyway, as you always told me.

Your abuse only seemed to get worse. Once you had my self-esteem on the floor, you made sure it stayed there. You made me sit at home whilst you went out until all hours, ignoring my calls, worrying if you were okay. I only knew you were fine when you would put pictures of yourself online, surrounded by other women. You would purposefully ignore me but reply to comments on social media. Remember the time I questioned you about this, and you slapped me? Or the time you didn't come home until 12 pm the next day and refused to talk to me, instead heading straight up to bed to sleep the whole day away. When you woke up, you gave me the silent treatment. The day after that, you headed to the doctors because you feared you'd caught an STI - but you accused me of giving it to you, not one of the many other women you slept with whilst you were with me. It's these things that pushed me further and further into a state of dissociative depression, unable to think or feel anything that was real - all I knew was dread, fear, and the sick feeling in the pit of my stomach. Yet, I still felt tied to you, and the thought of being without you made me feel so much pain and upset.

Fast forward to today, and the only thing I now feel for you is pity. It's so sad for me to think that you'll never ever know the feeling of genuine love, how to feel empathy or compassion, or ever be able to open up and truly feel close to another person.

If only you could understand just what it is that you lack, but you never will - because you don't want to face the idea that you *are* devoid of anything. Because you always shut down if you're confronted with the notion that you have to improve, change, or be better as a person, you revolt: you abuse, you gaslight and you manipulate instead of simply listening to those that care. Eventually, the ones that care won't be there. I do wonder what'll become of you then.

I can't even begin to imagine a world where there is no love, kindness, or genuine empathy. It staggers me to know that this is the world that you're living in. And I know first hand, whilst others show you such love, you're incapable of feeling its effects. You don't know that warm, comforting feeling of mutual love and respect. You'll never know that beauty.

Because of this, the only thing I have left for you is my pity.

Chapter Four - Can a Malignant Narcissist Ever Change?

After much debate on this topic, which has no definitive 'official' answer, myself and the countless other victims I've spoken to believe this to be the most accurate response to this question: *don't bank on it.*

I did hesitate in keeping this chapter in the book because people reforming and bettering themselves is something I don't like to count people out on. I think the majority of people who want to change for the better can do so - but I have one exception: *narcissists.*

Because of this contradictory belief, you may think that I'm being a bit unfair or undiplomatic towards malignant narcissists by saying I don't believe they can (in most cases) ever change - but narcissists and sociopaths are the *only* exceptions to my opinion that anyone can change.

I wanted to find a broader answer on this question, and I didn't want this chapter to just reflect my own opinion, so I sought out other victims' point of view on this often-asked question. I got a lofty response when I asked this question to people who've been in a relationship with a malignant narcissist: it was a resounding 'no' after 'no' flooding my inbox.

Whilst I'd ideally have liked a varying degree of answers for this chapter, the barrage of people who vehemently disagree that a malignant narcissist can ever change did help cement in my mind that I was correct in my original opinion. It helped solidify that, just like I'd always thought, a malignant narcissist is simply too far in the depths of their abusive, toxic and sadistic world wilderness to ever change. What's more, even if a narcissist *could* change - would they want to?

In order to come to my final conclusion of *'absolutely not - a malignant narcissist can never change',* I did a lot of back and forth in my head to try and break down this belief. I so much wanted to have faith that anyone can change and tried to find valid arguments to help me shoot down this opinion that I'd formed. So, any potential argument I could think of to help me explain why a malignant narcissist could change was promptly (but accurately) dismissed by the group I was conversing with about this question. Here is a breakdown of why a malignant narcissist will never change:

They Don't Want to Change

Abusive people are often rewarded by their toxic and abhorrent behavior and malignant narcissists are incapable of believing anything is wrong with them or the way they behave. Their intrinsic sense of superiority and consistent and lacking of empathy, readiness to exploit other people, as well as a very blatant lack of willingness to change their behavior, are all elemental to their extreme disorder.

As I mentioned earlier, malignant narcissists don't go to seek help voluntarily - they'll only go along with therapy if they have an agenda or manipulative trick in mind. In the group I pitched this question to, one former victim told us that her ex *did* end up going to therapy to seek help for his narcissism. However, this was ordered by the court after he was arrested for assaulting her, and it was the only way he would have avoided a harsher penalty. His acceptance to get help wasn't motivated by an authentic want to change, but rather to avoid punishment and *appear* to be wanting to better himself.

They're Not Abusive Because of Past Trauma - This Isn't a Valid Excuse for Abusive Behavior.

Mental illness is no joke, and as someone who has (and, in certain ways, always will) battled with mental health in the form of depression, I understand how misunderstood it can be and how difficult it is to live with. I understand the importance of prioritizing your mental health, and I have the utmost empathy for those who battle with their own mental health demons. However, I don't buy the notion that people with traumatic pasts have a hall pass to inflict terror and fear into others, and I don't like the misconception that all narcissists and abusers have had a traumatic upbringing; there is still no final, certain clinical verdict on what causes malignant narcissism, only theories; this, however, is one theory I'm inclined to disagree with.

Some abusers do come from troubled and traumatic backgrounds, just like some come from very privileged and comfortable upbringings with no traumatic experiences. And it goes without saying, there are millions and millions of survivors of malignant narcissistic abuse, cruel sociopaths, and psychopaths. These survivors, who've suffered horrific traumas at the hands of others, choose not to abuse as a result of their hurt. Inflicting abuse is a choice.

Much like any other disorder, it's often a mix of nature as well as nurture at the root of the issue - that's probably true for every human characteristic, both good and bad. Clinicians are uncertain of what causes narcissism, but there are a number of theories. Some theories suggest that those who have narcissistic traits tend to grow up in households where they've been brought up as overvalued, pandered to, spoiled, and raised to believe they should have a sense of entitlement. It's then theorized that these narcissistic traits, founded in childhood, can sometimes later turn into full-on narcissism in adulthood.

The need that many of us have to rationalize traumatic, abusive behavior based on a story of past traumas can cause abuse victims to repeatedly minimize their own emotional pain, constantly excusing their tormentor's behavior whilst still looping around the abuse cycle. Additionally, because malignant narcissists have such a limited emotional radar, and for the most part, can only experience shallow emotions, they don't feel the same empathy you would expect from someone who has been through trauma.

The victims of malignant narcissists certainly endure horrible abuse and are undeniably traumatized by them. Not only can I vouch for this myself, but I've spoken with lots of narcissism survivors who've endured the trauma of abuse at the hands of a malignant narcissist. Some were abused by narcissists who came from happy, nourishing, loving families with an idyllic upbringing. Those who are full-on psychopaths could have been born like that, and so their upbringing would have no bearing on their abusive ways at all.

It's important to remember to have empathy for the traumas that survivors of abuse have endured - not the perpetrators. Most abuse survivors chose not to abuse other people, instead, they allow their traumas to guide them on how to treat others with more empathy and respect.

Chapter Five - Anna's Story: I Feel Helpless

Anna was with her abusive, violent, narcissistic ex for five years, and has been free of him for about a year. Her story goes to show that, even when you're free of the malignant narc, their abuse has a lasting effect. Anna has come on in leaps and bounds since she finally rid herself of her abusive ex, but she still has a long way to go when it comes to rebuilding her inner strength and self-esteem. I wanted to include her story so that in the future, Anna can see just how far she's come, and I also wanted to show other victims that it's so common to feel this way after an abusive relationship:

My ex was a malignant narcissist - there are no doubts in my mind about this, as I've researched this topic so much after hearing about it. So many of the traits he had go hand in hand with malignant narcissism, sociopathic behavior and often psychopathic actions. If I had to assign one disorder to summarize him, it would be malignant narcissism. After all, a malignant often has traits of other disorders, which certainly describes my ex.

If I'm totally honest, I'm struggling quite a bit at the moment. I'm not healed, even though I see lots of people who've recovered so much quicker than me, I'm not hopeful - I feel so lost and helpless, even though I'm no longer with my abusive ex.

As I write this, tomorrow is the one year anniversary of the exact date I finally went to the police and got the abuse recorded and documented. I'm also nine days away from the date he finally left my home. I'm still trying to heal, I'm really, really trying. I think I'm on the road to healing, but feeling just 'okay' seems like a world away right now. Last winter I had to have seven weeks off my job as a social worker, because I had a total nervous breakdown. Right now, I'm back at work, and I've been back for a few months now - everything seems to be going okay. Some days I feel free, other days I feel such a heavy burden of panic, anxiety, and a dread of the unknown. Logically, I know I'm free, and I'm trying to plan my future.

I'm trying to accept that my ex wasn't 'the one', although I find this hard. I've never felt the way I do about anyone, the way I felt about him. I can't imagine feeling that way ever again. I feel like I will be alone, for a long time, if not forever. Some days I have an overwhelming feeling to speak to him again, even though I know it's wrong. Towards the end of the relationship, the abuse was more than just lies, manipulation and nasty verbal attacks - he began to physically abuse me. I know he'd do it again, because he sucked me back in a few weeks after he initially left. I'd managed to get a restraining order, but he kept calling the house and he told me he still had his key, so I was totally afraid. But, still, a big part of me yearned to have him back - I was all alone and afraid. So, after a couple of weeks, I relented - I let him back in the house. He seemed sad, and lost, and I let him stay a few nights. He kept asking me to withdraw my police report, and lift the restraining order, which I eventually tried to do.

I called the specially trained officer who had been assigned to me and told her I wanted to withdraw my report and take away the restraining order. It was as if she immediately knew he was back in my life, even though I lied to her and told her that I just didn't want the hassle - but she could tell I was being pressured by my ex. I just wanted peace, and if that meant retracting what I told the police, then so be it. However, the officer told me that it didn't work like that - she told me that my safety was paramount, and whilst she couldn't stop me from returning to my abusive ex, it was in my best interest to keep the restraining order. She also told me that they needed to keep my statement on file, and it wasn't as easy as simply retracting it.

When I told my ex this, he hit the roof.

He accused me of lying, of just saying I couldn't get my report to police wiped off file. I pleaded and begged with him, and told him I really did try to get them to forget what I'd told them. But he wouldn't listen. He dragged me from the kitchen to the living room by the hair and spent what felt like an eternity screaming, punching, slapping and verbally humiliating me. This probably went on for like an hour, and I managed to call the police when he left the room. I locked myself in the downstairs bathroom until they arrived, by which point my ex had fled. This episode proved to me that he would never change - if anything, he was only going to get worse.

As you can probably tell, today is one of my 'bad days'; I'm not always this down about everything. Some days, I feel like I'm on the right track, others (like today), I feel like my ex has ruined me. I feel like I'll never be the person I was again. Everyone says I'll be me again, in time. They say I'll be stronger, wiser and better, but that just makes me feel worse, because all I think is, *'how?'*

Chapter Six - The Dangers of a Malignant Narcissist: The Effects of Malignant Abuse

You don't come out of a relationship with a malignant narcissist unscathed. You will have scars and you will have effects that will stay with you for a long time. And why wouldn't you? You've been emotionally violated, lied to, manipulated and cruelly played with for the entertainment and amusement of the narcissist. Not only that, you've likely been gaslighted so much that you probably don't have the greatest faith in your own decision making anymore. The chances are, you've also had to deal with violence throughout the duration of your relationship, as malignant narcs are prone to dishing out aggression with their fists as well as their mouths.

The fact that you were cruelly duped into believing the person you met and fell for was the person you would be in a relationship with is a tough, and it's a heartbreaking pill to swallow. The life you'd imagined you'd have (and were told you would have) ended up being a huge lie; broken and shattered to the point that it's almost laughable that you thought you could ever have that.

Add to this that your self-worth and sense of self has been chipped at until there's little to nothing left there anymore, and you have the foundations for the horrible side-effects of malignant narcissistic abuse.

MALIGNANT NARCISSISM

The relationship destroyed my identity, my sense of safety and comfort and my idea of what love meant was flipped on its head. As I mentioned earlier, whilst I was in an abusive relationship for seven years, the after-effects that I had to deal with in the aftermath of this meant I was still reeling from the abuse for longer than the relationship itself lasted.

I'm going to outline the effects that victims of malignant narcissistic abuse are often left with, even if they're no longer in the abusive relationship. I hope that this next segment, like the last chapter, will offer some points that resonate with you and give you a deeper understanding of how the toxicity of malignant narcissism effects those who have endured it.

You Use Dissociation as a Survival / Defence / Coping Mechanism

At the very core of trauma - more specifically, trauma caused by abuse - is disassociation. This word is referring to the emotional and physical detachment you begin to feel to the world around you. Not only this, but disassociation can also leave you with a disrupted sense of consciousness, which in turn, gives you a disrupted sense of self. Dissociation, although a coping mechanism to deal with the trauma of abuse, leaves you fragmented and numb.

Becoming numb after torrents of abuse, physical or mental, is a common dissociation tactic victims will use to survive. Even in the face of horrific acts of abuse, a person who has disassociated themselves so much can be emotionally numb to the vile things they're subjected to.

When I was in the midst of my abusive relationship, dissociation took over. I was like a zombie, just a surviving entity, but with no life in me. Vile words that once hurt so deeply became a part of the everyday vocabulary I was used to hearing. Awaiting accusations or being blamed for things I'd never imagine doing became part of my life - I accepted these things simply as my way of life.

Our mind uses dissection to protect us, to prevent us from any further emotional trauma. Whilst this does serve as a coping mechanism for the short term when you're in an abusive relationship, dissociation becomes your new reality, and it's a dangerous place to be. Once you've been there a while, it's hard to get out - after all, what's outside of your disassociative state is something you've learned to dread.

You Chronically Walk on Eggshells

Even after an abusive relationship with a malignant narcissist, you'll likely find that you still walk on eggshells. This is because you're afraid of triggering something that'll make you relive the trauma of the things you've been through. Things other people wouldn't bat an eyelid at, you'll see as potential threats. Certain types of people, certain places and activities will be seen as a danger; they may pose a threat to you because they remind you of the abuse that you try desperately to avoid repeating. Even if these people are your family or friends, you may still sense danger when you're around them.

You'll find that you're watching what you're saying or doing, trying to avoid verbal punishment or making yourself a target of their anger. You'll also avoid making yourself someone who could be the target of someone else's envy - you don't want to provoke any kind of attention that results in abuse, so you'll do anything to lay low, even going as far as covering up any achievements you may have accomplished.

I was always perpetually afraid and anxious that I would say or do something that would provoke my ex into being vile and wicked towards me. I'd do whatever I could to fly beneath his radar, avoiding his wrath at all costs.

However, after leaving the relationship, I came to understand that nothing I did or didn't do would stop me from becoming the primary target whenever my ex felt the need to attack me. I was his emotional and physical punching bag, and no matter how hard I tried to avoid confrontation when he decided it was time to play - it was time to play.

After I escaped the relationship, I realized that I was unconsciously extending this 'people pleasing' characteristic to other people who weren't my ex. The people pleaser I'd become meant that I was weak when it came to setting boundaries. I couldn't be assertive or voice my own opinion for fear of triggering a verbal assault. I found this to be especially true when it came to people or situations that resembled my ex and the relationship. Certain people, without intending to or realizing, struck fear right through me with the things they'd say or do that reminded me of my abusive relationship.

Your Basic Needs Are Pushed Aside to Benefit Others

Before I was entangled in an abusive relationship, I was full of hopes, dreams, and aspirations. I was excited about what the world had to offer and what I could offer the world - I was young, peppy, and ready to take on life.

It's funny how things can change in such a short space of time.

Once I'd became involved with my ex, the old me was flipped on her head. My life's purpose became to fulfill the needs of my partner. I didn't have my own agenda anymore, and my entire life revolved around him. This was a painful irony to digest because, at one point, my ex made me feel like his life revolved around me - until he decided that was no longer the case, and that I was better utilized as his permanent source of narcissistic supply.

This may be the case for you, too - you once had friends, hobbies, goals, and dreams, all of which have been placed on the backburner whilst you pander to your abuser. Your basic needs are pushed to one side in order to completely satisfy the narcissist, making sure they feel content.

This, as you may have come to understand, is a fruitless endeavor. Nothing you do for the malignant narcissist will ever satisfy them or make them content.

Your Physical Health Reflects Your Mental Health

Your physical wellbeing during an abusive relationship almost always reflects your mental wellbeing - even if you don't see it that way at the time. For a long time, I found it hard to look back at pictures of myself from when I was with my abuser. I was thin, gaunt and had dead eyes. My hair was unkempt. My clothes were unflattering. I was constantly sleepy, always wanting to be in bed asleep. When I was asleep, at least, there was no fear of abuse (most of the time this was the case, anyway).

All I wanted to do was cry, but I was no numb that the tears just didn't come. My stomach was always in knots, my mind was always racing but never thinking properly. I aged possibly fifteen years during the seven I was in this demeaning relationship. My heart would palpitate, my nerves were always shot and I was so unfit due to having zero desire to exercise.

As I said, I found it hard to look at pictures like this for a long time. I think that's because, whilst I was with my ex, I had no idea I looked so bad. I thought I was holding it together, that I was hiding my pain well. From those pictures, it clear to see that I was far from well.

Now may be a good time to reflect on your own physical health as a result of the abuse you are or were enduring. It can be so easily neglected until you're forced to confront it when it gets worse and worse. Before it gets to that point, it's worth taking stock of your physical wellbeing. Are you sleeping enough? Are you sleeping too much or too little? Are your eating habits healthy? Do you exercise enough? Are there any hobbies you've stopped but would like to get back into?

When you're at your lowest ebb, it can be hard to even *want* to think about your physical health; perhaps you're even at the point where you don't care. I remember being there, too. However, your physical health is an external representation of your emotional health - the two are linked in more ways than I thought imaginable. Make sure you're taking care of your physical health too.

You're Extremely Mistrustful

Mistrust can be ingrained so deeply after an abusive relationship that almost everyone you meet poses a potential threat. You might find that you're dubious and apprehensive about the true intentions of other people, and you're skeptical that the things they say or do are genuine. This is because you've already experienced the heartache and trauma of someone you once trusting turning out to be someone who hurt you so cruelly by revealing themselves to be a vile bully.

This is more than just your usual, cautionary perception of others that we all experience from time to time - it's a pervasive, serious mistrust that other people will let you down, hurt you and potentially abuse you. A healthy, cautionary approach to others becomes a hypervigilance that sees every new person as a threat to you and your wellbeing.

This mistrust, whilst brought on from the negative experiences of an abusive relationship, was also directly instilled into you by the abuser themselves. They gaslighted you so much to believe that your thoughts and experiences were invalid, you don't trust anyone... least of all yourself.

You Isolate Yourself

Being isolated by your abuser is something that happens over time in an abusive relationship, but it often leads to the point where you no longer need the abuser's input in this - you simply begin to isolate yourself. The coercion and manipulation of the narcissist are no longer required, you're happy to do the job of isolating yourself, without them prodding you along.

This is often because isolation means you don't have to feel the shame, embarrassment or judgment from those outside of the relationship. If a friend is becoming concerned about you, it's easier to cut them off than explain your situation. If a work colleague is getting too close, you'll cut contact before your abuser catches wind and punishes you. If family members comment on how ill you look, you'd rather not speak to them at all than explain your complex, abusive relationship to them - after all, they'd never understand.

Victim-blaming is rife in today's culture, which serves to keep the downtrodden and abused unheard. Victims of abuse don't want to have to go through more trauma by being disbelieved, judged and invalidated by others. It's much easier to isolate yourself than it is to face those traumatic possibilities.

The fear of being misunderstood, believed or helped is enough to make you withdraw from others, not to mention the fear your abuser instills in you preventing you from having connections with people in the first place.

Chapter Seven - Clare's Story: It's Your Loss

I must have given off 'weak' vibes when my narcissistic ex appeared in my life. I'd just lost my mother around ten months prior, and it hit me hard, so he must have sensed the vulnerability on me (narcissists have a habit of doing that. To them, weakness equals opportunity).

He very quickly told me that we were soulmates - destined to meet, because he was my 'saviour', he 'fixed me' and 'made me the person I am today' (all his words). It's funny - I think back now to his manipulative words and I cringe for him. I always wondered, how could we be soulmates? It's such a bold and committed statement to say to someone, yet when I never seemed to understand how to make my 'one in a billion' husband happy. He always made me feel like he was doing me a favor by being with me like it was a chore or a task for him - something he was doing to be a good Samaritan. But, then he could contradict this with his big, bold statements of love. I never knew how to play his game right; the rules were made up by him, and because they changed so frequently, I was never able to keep up. Before I knew it, I was constantly reminded about how idiotic, bad and incompetent I was. He would tell me one thing one day, then completely deny it the next. When this happens so frequently, you begin to really believe you're going crazy. It doesn't help when you're told on a bi-daily basis that you *are* crazy.

Throughout the course of my toxic, doomed relationship, I did a lot of things to work on myself - in an attempt to figure out exactly what was so wrong with me. I needed to find out just what it was about me that made my partner treat me so horribly. I thought it must have been me that triggered his nasty streak because he was so different with most other people.

My ex worked away a lot, and had to take lots of trips to other cities for his job. Whilst he was away, I started to become really concerned about the frequency and length of his trips. Of course, my sense of what was real, what was right, and what was wrong was now skewed - he'd gaslighted me so much I wasn't sure about much anymore. However, my perceptions and gut instincts weren't completely dead - I still had strong suspicions about what he was doing on these 'trips'. It did get harder, however, to keep trusting my own gut, because the fog he had installed in my brain was only getting harder to see through.

For over a decade, I put up with his screaming, shouting, and yelling and what eventually became physical assaults toward me. I'd always defended my adoration and fidelity towards him, but it was beyond heartbreaking to never get that back in return. After 13 years together with my abusive husband, who now wasn't the man I fell in love with, I felt more like a shell - an empty vessel that was merely just surviving, not really living at all.

My trampled soul was totally crushed, barely alive. I remember telling one of my closest friends that I felt like I was dead on the inside, but this was frustrating because they couldn't really understand what I meant - they all had healthy, loving relationships. Whilst she listened to me and took in what I was saying, I could tell she couldn't empathize because she had no clue what this felt like.

Eventually, I became so broken and non-responsive that my husband left me for someone else - his new 'soulmate'. This, coupled with the really good divorce settlement he got (with zero regards to fairness or decency) meant I was at rock bottom for a little while. It felt like I was born to be life's punching bag.

Now, it's been around a year since the divorce settled. He lies about his income, which means he doesn't give the kids half as much as they deserve, but they seem to know what kind of person he is without me having to tell them. They saw me at rock bottom, and they witnessed the hell he put me through.

Once I began to heal, I came to understand that my ex will continue to live such an empty, toxic, angry life of suspicion and distrust. The kids, for all they can see right through him, are still caught in his web of toxicity and manipulation. If they're on his good side, he lavishes them with gifts and money. If they step out of line, or challenge his frail ego, they get nothing - not even his attention. He's not afraid to give the kids his stony silent treatment. Of course, he can offer them what I can't - money, new gadgets, fancy things... and that's what teenagers are attracted to. I just hope that, as they grow older, my kids remember who will always be there for them, regardless of how many gifts, wads of cash or fancy holidays my ex throws at them.

Whilst I was married to my ex, he often told me how I wasn't good enough at anything. All I ever really wanted from him was to be appreciated for the things I did; rarely was I thanked for all I did and all I gave up for him. It's like it was just expected. I just wanted, even just every now and again, some appreciation. I never got that from him.

He also made up nasty, mean nicknames for all of my friends. He always made really negative comments and jibes about each one of my friends, like none of them were good enough to be someone he had in his life. He looked down his nose at the people who had always been there for me, through thick and thin. But, he had zero friends of his own - at least, he had no male friends.

He also found it hard to keep a job, I think. He seemed to keep changing companies really frequently, around once a year, sometimes more frequently than that. It made me quite concerned. He would come home after a work trip, and not go back for a few weeks, and I eventually asked him, 'Did you get fired?' Whilst he denied ever being fired, there was always a different job. Sometimes I think he lied about the title of his jobs too, because each one seemed to have a better job title than the last.

Since the demise of my marriage, the biggest hurdle has been finding the strength to co-parent. My ex is a monster, a vile human being, and a disgusting manipulator. But, he's the father of my children. I do think he loves them, in his own way. In an ideal world, I'd never have had children with him, but I adore my kids with all my heart, and I'd be lost without them. Whilst it can be frustrating, maddening and sometimes unbearable having him as a co-parent, I have to remind myself that as long as I'm providing a stable, loving, and warm home for my children, that's what matters - that they know true love, and they know they can come to me about anything. They won't grow up to be like their father, as long as I'm there.

To get through the tough, emotionally draining times, I learned how to breathe. I now regularly practice slow breathing with intention. I seek calmness and clarity. Talking to other victims gave me that, too. I'm now in a much healthier place, a much happier place, and I have so much lost time to catch up on; so many places, people, and things I avoided during my abusive relationship are now mine to explore. And I intend to do just that.

Chapter Eight - The 'Perfect' Traits of the Prey of Malignant Narcissists

"Nice people don't necessarily fall in love with nice people."

As I mentioned at the start of this book, a malignant narcissist doesn't seek a nervous, socially unaware wallflower to be their prey. The stereotypical victim template isn't true for most abusers or victims, especially those who have suffered at the hands of a malignant narcissist. For the seven years I was in this abusive relationship, I doubted all of the things I was so sure of before.

Maybe I wasn't as smart as I thought I was, seeing as I didn't see through the facade this man put on whilst courting me. Perhaps I wasn't as career-focused as I had always stated I was, as I had let my work ethic slip and avoided chasing my dream career. I'd always been outgoing and liked meeting new people, but I found myself avoiding making friends or even speaking to the ones I had.

Of course, these were all things that were a direct result of the relationship I was in. I *was* clever, capable of achievement and outgoing, but my abusive partner had clipped my wings and stopped me exhibiting any of those traits that I once held so dear.

People who were or are victims of a malignant narcissist all tend to have a similar set of characteristics. We're all very similar in nature and carry a lot of identical traits. These traits are golden for a malignant narcissist; if they see a person with the traits I'm going to outline below, a malignant sees opportunity. They see a chance to seize power and obtain a full gauge of narcissistic supply from that person.

The traits that I'm going to outline, I need to stress, aren't bad. **They're wonderful**.

They're the kind of characteristics that would make the world so much nicer, kinder and full of empathy if narcissistic vampires weren't intercepting it and using it to their own manipulative advantage. Please think of these traits as **qualities**; because that's what they are. The purpose of this chapter is to help you understand what the malignant narcissist saw in you that made you more susceptible to their abuse and to help you see the traits that malignant leeches look for in a victim.

Resilient

A malignant narcissist will actively seek out a resilient partner who has incredible 'bounce-back-ability'. On the surface, it would seem that a malignant seeking out a resilient partner would be counterintuitive - after all, a resilient person is often also seen as 'tough' or 'difficult' when trying to manipulate. However, in this instance, the resilience of the victim comes in the form of being able to withstand a lot of emotional pain and hurt. Very often, the abuser will seek out someone who has had an abusive or troubled childhood. This means the victim comes pre-installed with the emotional resilience the abuser requires. Childhood abuse survivors, like myself, have an uncanny ability to withstand a huge amount of pain and suffering without giving up. We remain hopeful, even in the direst of situations. It's a coping mechanism. And it's also a huge attraction for a malignant narcissist.

If you have a strong, resilient nature, then I encourage you to never change that, no matter how much people chip away at you. Keep that beautiful quality, against all odds. It'll end up being one of your greatest assets.

However, when you're in the clutches of a malignant narcissist, this wonderful quality becomes something the abuser uses to keep you in their snare. Your resilience becomes something the narcissist will use against you to keep you in the abusive relationship. They know you're tough, and they know you won't give up. You'll take the abuse, and bounce back up, ready to take some more. Like a human bobo doll, you'll get knocked down by the narcissist and you'll pop right back up again. Of course, the narc will happily (and with great pleasure) knock you right back down yet again.

It's a constant cycle that people with lower emotional resilience just couldn't take.

Our 'fighter' mindset is something we've become accustomed to, and we train ourselves to fight for what we want. We want to be loved and we want to feel safe, and we fight for that, even if it means enduring horrific abuse at the hands of a malignant narcissist. The resilience of the victim can also be used as a way to gauge the love they have for their abuser; they can sometimes use the amount of abuse they put up with as a bargaining tool with their tormentor: 'I must really love this person because I put up with so much cruelty from them.'

High Levels of Integrity

A morally absent malignant narcissist seeks out a partner with a wealth of integrity. This is because individuals that possess the traits associated with integrity offer up a heap of characteristics that the narcissist can exploit.

People who have a strong moral compass are less likely to 'give up' on a relationship. People with good morals and trustworthiness are more likely to try and work on any problems within the relationship and be more inclined to ask themselves how **they** can improve to help the partnership flourish. In a healthy and loving relationship, these characteristics are undoubtedly necessary, but in a relationship with a malignant, they are used to benefit the narcissist.

The traits associated with high levels of integrity are a far cry from the narcissist's lack of empathy and remorse. The abuser will use their victims' strong morals against them, making the victim feel obliged to put up with the abuse out of moral responsibility towards their abuser.

Empathetic

On the narcissist's list of 'perfect prey characteristics', empathy scores highly. A malignant narcissist requires a huge amount of narcissistic supply, and they won't get that from someone who doesn't offer up plentiful amounts of empathy. Those who have an empathetic nature are more inclined to give the narcissist the attention, praise and resources they need in order to top up their narcissistic fuel to the brim.

The malignant will feed off of their victims' abundance of empathy in order to get the power and control they require. Whilst the trait of empathy is a beautiful, empowering and loving attribute, the narcissist takes it and uses it to their wicked advantage. The ability the victim has to want to understand others' feelings is something the abuser will use against them to disempower them; it's a ploy to keep them in the cycle of abuse.

As an empathetic individual, the victim will be more than willing to want to understand the narcissist's perspective and understand why they behave the way they do. By being so willing to *want* to understand the narcissist, the victim is offering their abuser something they rely on in order to maintain the control and power they so desperately crave. An understanding partner who really feels for their significant other is susceptible to falling for their abusers sob stories and pity ploys, particularly after an abusive incident.

The narcissist will use tales of woe to lure their victim back into their grip, and may even use them as a way of apologizing for their behavior (which isn't an apology; it's an excuse).

A malignant narcissist knows that if they tell sob stories, their partner will strive to use this as a way to explain away their vile behavior. At the very core of a narcissist's ideal prey is an empathetic nature - without this, they wouldn't be able to use their hard-luck stories as an excuse for their unrelenting toxicity.

An abundance of empathy from the victim means a forgiving spirit and sympathetic manner is something they offer regardless of the disgusting and horrific treatment their abuser puts them through.

The malignant will appeal to the empathy of their victim to help them swerve accountability for the poor treatment they bestow upon them.

The Ability to Love Deeply

The quality of being able to love deeply and unconditionally is a characteristic that, in the right hands, can offer you the greatest feelings life can offer. An abundance of reciprocated love in a trustworthy and honest relationship can leave you feeling on cloud nine, no matter how many years you've been with your partner. This means that the ability to love deeply is a quality that can bring you profuse happiness... unless it slips into the wrong hands.

Being able to love sentimentally and deeply is a trait that malignant narcissist can sense a mile off, and it's an integral characteristic they look for in a partner because it can be used to 'groom' them into a false sense of security. The malignant will appeal to their victims' desire and ability to love by 'love-bombing' them in the early stages of the relationship. This sets the scene for the narcissist to secure the trust and adoration of their victim. As I mentioned earlier, a narcissist doesn't outright expose themselves as the cruel, sadistic and aggressive person they truly are - they lay the fake foundations of romance first.

Whilst they are cold, calculating and manipulative, a malignant narcissist is also very smart, and they know that their victim will romanticize about the loved up beginnings of their relationship when the abuse kicks in. As well as being a way to keep the victim in their cycle of abuse, it's also a sick way for the narc to gain pleasure from the torment the put their victim through - they know that the toying and toing and froing of emotions will be destroying their victim. This sick way of deriving power and pleasure is how the malignant ensures they're 'on top' in the relationship.

The narc can act as if they love intensely and passionately until they begin to withdraw that love, affection, and comfort. This withdrawal is done completely deliberately, knowing their victim will be craving the 'soulmate' they fell in love with. They know they'll be leaving their victim confused, desperate to please and depleted of their self-worth, hopelessly chasing the narc to regain the same love they were used to receiving. This, in turn, tops up the narcissistic supply

Dedicated

A dedicated person will throw themselves into the relationship and follow through on their promises. They feel obliged to make sure their actions match their words. Dedicated people tend to also be conscientious, making their choices based on their morals and their conscience first and foremost. Because of this, they expect the same from their partner; the one who says that they love and adore them.

And why shouldn't that be expected of someone who tells you such intimate things?

In most instances, that most certainly *should be expected* as a basic expectation of your partner - but you can kiss that goodbye when you enter a relationship with a malignant narcissist. Instead, the narcissist will see their victims dedicated and conscientious nature to exploit that quality in order to best serve their own nefarious wants and needs.

A malignant narcissist knows all too well that a dedicated person is also someone who wants to fulfill their 'obligation' in the relationship, and that also means serving the narc and tending to their needs, even if it means neglecting their own. This unwavering sense of dedication to the relationship means the victim will even place themselves in harm's way to make sure their partner is pacified.

*

The malignant narc, as they interact more and more with their victim, carefully and meticulously assesses the persona of their chosen prey. This enables the narc to come up with a bigger picture of how their victim thinks and what their core values and characteristics are, which helps them understand their weaknesses and insecurities.

One could also describe a malignant narcissist as an intense student of human behavior, using their findings of these observations to better hurt, torment and humiliate their victims.

You may have gone through this chapter and thought that many of the traits - or qualities - I've described fit you accurately. I hope it helps you better understand that a) it's not your fault that you're in a relationship with a narcissist, and b) you're full of good qualities that unfortunately makes you perfect prey for the narc.

Chapter Nine - Trauma Bonded to Your Abuser

I wanted to dedicate a chapter to go through something that's a huge part of abusive, narcissistic relationships, but something that's also rarely talked about: the traumatic bond that victims often have with their abuser. This term may or may not be something you've come across before, but I'll explain what it means in this chapter. I don't think there are enough 'real life' stories of people being trauma bonded to a narcissist out there; there are mostly just big-news stories of people being abducted and how they became so trauma bonded to their captor that they didn't want them brought to justice.

Trauma bonding also takes place in abusive relationships, both violent and verbal, and I'd like to go a bit more in-depth about this and give some insight into how it may have affected you.

You may be wondering, *so what is narcissistic trauma bonding*? *How does this come about?*

Trauma bonding is the bond that forms when the victim experiences repeated intense emotional encounters with their abuser. It can be compared to Stockholm Syndrome, which sees feelings of trust or affection felt by a victim towards their abuser, often in cases of kidnapping or hostage situations. The two run parallel to each other in that the victim is being held emotionally captive, either via emotional or physical abuse - oftentimes it's both.

Trauma bonding is an unwavering loyalty to the person who is destroying them. It's almost like you're a willing participant to the destruction because it means appeasing and pleasing your abuser. Being trauma bonded can mean the following:

- No matter how much you're let down, lied to or accept non-performance, you still believe or hold hope that this will change, regardless of the evidence and past performance that suggests otherwise.

- You're not as seemingly affected or disturbed by an event or situation that most people would be unsettled by. If others have witnessed or know about the horrible things that've been said to you or done to you, but you don't seem as fazed by it as they do, this is a strong sign that that trauma bond is in full effect.

- You feel completely stuck in your situation because you feel like you can't do anything about it - you accept your fate as not being in your own hands.

- You've likely tried to change your abuser, to no avail. Any addictions, toxic behaviors or unhealthy vices they may have will have been something you've attempted to help them with.

- No matter your lack of trust, inability to be yourself and constant fear in the relationship, you can't detach yourself. Even if you feel resentful or dislike towards your abuser, you can't imagine life without them. Leaving or being without them seem impossible.

- You feel like you're being emotionally crushed and tormented when you're not with them; you long for them so much it hurts. The mere idea of being without them permanently makes you uncertain how you'd survive.

The reason we become trauma bonded to someone who's so cruel, manipulative and vile towards us is because the malignant narcissist has created a perfect breeding ground for a trauma bond to develop.

The right environment is one that includes inconsistency, emotional complexity, high levels of intensity and *a promise*. This promise may not even be a verbal one from the abuser, it could be the promise of hope; that things will change and the person you're with eventually revert back to the person you met. The perfect environment for a trauma bond to develop also includes manipulation, whereby the victim will tolerate this behavior in order to receive the anticipated payout of *the promise*; of course, this never arrives.

I'll outline below some of the classic side effects of trauma bonding:

You Feel Addicted to Your Abuser

Even though they make you feel low, unworthy and downright broken, the familiarity of your abuser gives you a sense of comfort. When you're not with your abuser, your entire being feels like it aches for them - you're desperate to just be with them. Your entire world as you knew it has changed to fit around them, and it's all you know.

This addiction causes you to neglect yourself. You don't sleep as much as you ought to, your energy is used on trying to appease your abuser. You yearn for them, regardless of how awfully they treat you. This unhealthy addiction sees you trying, with everything you've got, to get them to reciprocate your feelings. This, in turn, will also be a way to stop some of the abuse from occurring.

I felt completely addicted to my abuser. For a while, I felt uncomfortable saying this; it sounded like I was admitting that I enjoyed the abuse, or at least that's what I thought. I've now come to terms with a lot of the feelings I experienced during my abusive relationship, and this feeling of addiction is a very common one in cases of trauma bonding.

I'd be anxious when he wasn't around, I'd spend my days needing to be with him, I'd do everything in my power to make sure his needs were met and all the while I'd be foregoing my own needs and wants.

You Yearn to Please Them No Matter What

Regardless of the pain and terror inflicted upon you by the narcissist, trauma bonding means you'll strive to please your abuser no matter what. You'll be loyal to them to a fault, even if you're not getting back anything but pain in return.

A narcissist will terrorize and hurt their victim, often knowing that they won't have to deal with the consequences of their actions because their victim will be ready to take them back anyway. All it would take is perhaps a hint of attention or possibly even a little fake remorse; their victim will be prepared to go through it all again.

You'll bend over backward to make sure your abuser is pacified, even if that means defending them to others. I recall a co-worker of mine trying to give me a reality check about my relationship, as he'd seen what had been happening - he noticed I'd retreated into my shell, that I was withdrawn, that I wasn't the person he remembered when we first met. He'd also witnessed some of the paranoid behavior my abusive ex would exhibit, like turning up at my work to check up on me or calling my work to ask for me to make sure I was there.

The things he said to me - that I was in a toxic relationship with someone who didn't respect me - were all true. He could see the harm this relationship was doing to me. He knew I was drained, he could tell from my demeanor and the way I'd changed from a chatty, open and reliable worker to the complete opposite of that. However, I wasn't ready to face the truth. Even if, deep down, I knew he was one hundred percent right, I wasn't ready to accept that. The truth was too daunting. It was unfamiliar and filled with the horrifying idea that I'd need to leave my ex. I wasn't ready.

I was committed to investing everything I had into making the relationship work. To accept the notion that it was all in vain was too much for me to handle, so I chose not to. Instead, I remembered the person my ex was at the beginning of the relationship and tried my best to get that person to return. To accept who my ex really was wasn't something I felt emotionally stable enough to do.

You Become Self Destructive

The very nature of a trauma bond is having a distorted perception of reality. You have a skewed view of not only your abuser but also of yourself. Your self-esteem and self-worth have both been pummeled to the point of barely existing. Because of this, self-destruction and self-sabotage become the norm, even if you are subconsciously doing it - it's something that's been programmed into you by your abuser. You're not worthy of peacefulness or comfort. Therefore, your natural reflex is to be self-destructive.

This entrapment by your abuser instills a sense of sheer helplessness into you, which is fuelled by the feeling of inability to ever be free of your abuser. Often, cutting the emotional cord to your abuser is something most trauma bonded individuals are unable to do, even if the resources and options to break free are there and available; that shows how emotionally tethered victims of abuse can become to their abuser.

You've Lowered Your Standards Gradually and Have Forgotten Your Worth

From a once optimistic, self-assured and somewhat confident person, this abusive relationship turned me into the complete opposite. As the relationship became more and more toxic, I felt more and more unworthy and began to fight for the attention and affection I once received so freely. The ways in which I pursued my abuser's affections were derogatory to myself, although, at the time, that didn't matter: all that mattered was him.

I was convinced by him, both outrightly and by suggestion, that I wasn't enough. I felt like I was in competition with everything and everyone else, and lowered my standards to make sure I was approved of.

This subsequently meant that, as well as battling the feelings of invisibility and worthlessness, a big chunk of my energy was spent trying to claw back the love I craved from my abuser. I lowered my standards completely to do this and accepted treatment that validated what I'd been trained to think: that I was worthless.

Trauma bonding means the victim lowers their expectations, needs, and standards to meet the toxic relationship they're in because they'd rather deal with this than the trauma of leaving their abuser.

You're Aware They're Manipulative, Deceptive and a Liar, But Letting Go Seems Impossible

I'm rational and always felt like I'm good at reading people, and I've always been able to 'see through' the fraudsters and liars. This may sound like you, too - and you're very likely right about yourself. You most probably are very good at weeding out the deceptive people and are aware when someone is trying to play mind games with you.

Just like I was, you're also very aware of all the things your abuser is, but you can't seem to let go. You're aware you're being mistreated, lied to, manipulated and devalued.

I felt so much anger about this; I was annoyed at myself, my seemingly hopeless situation and did feel some resentment towards my abuser for making me feel like this. Of course, I didn't show this externally, I kept it inside for fear of upsetting him or making him withdraw affection from me. This anger remained unresolved for a while after the relationship ended, and it took me some time before I stopped blaming myself for the toxic relationship.

Trauma bonding occurs in extremely abusive relationships because even toxic relationships still have their moments of 'normality', which ensures the victim keeps hold of their hope that things will be 'normal' all the time, one day. The strength of this traumatic connection is only strengthened by the hope that the victim retains of finally reaching normality.

Chapter Ten - Escaping the Narcissist

Leaving a malignant narcissist, as you may know yourself, isn't easy. I'm not just referring to the actual act of leaving either; the thought alone can be enough to strike fear into you. Narcissist's instill dread, doubt, and uncertainty into you in order to keep you where they want you, and this makes the idea of leaving something that's hard to even *think* about thinking about.

The road to safety and freedom is blocked by the malignant narc, as they guard that path ominously and carefully.

The thought of heading that way can send shivers down your spine. This is why so many victims stay with their abuser; because of the threat of the emotional or physical repercussions, they'll be faced with if they try to leave. A lot of time, the abuser will use finances as a way to stop their victim leaving also.

As well as this, there is also the lesser talked about reason many of us freeze when confronted with the idea of leaving our abuser: we love them. To rip yourself away from someone you love and care for is just about the hardest thing you can do, even when you know it's the right thing to do.

If you're anything like I was, you've daydreamed dozens upon dozens of times about bundling all of your cash together and escaping for a better life. Only, I didn't have any money. And I had nowhere to go. Like a lot of victims of abuse, I felt tied to my situation. I didn't feel like I could leave: emotionally, physically, mentally, or financially. However, those are simply roadblocks that the narc has put in place to stop you from prizing yourself away from their steely grip.

In this chapter, I want to talk about the pathway to freedom; how to ready your mind so you can rid yourself of the narcissist and find the peace and understanding that everyone (especially *you*) deserves.

If you're reading this, thinking to yourself, *'I know I ought to leave them - but I don't think I'll ever be capable of doing that'*, then this chapter is for you. Even if you feel utterly trapped, with zero belief that you'll ever leave, then I think this chapter will be of benefit to you. It's dedicated to building the mental foundations you need to mentally leave the malignant narc, which sets you up for the time when you feel like you can finally be free of your abuser.

Because of the nature of malignant narcissism, and the type of abuse it forces victims to endure, we need to go through a set of mental stages before we can detach ourselves from the malignant narc. Once we begin our way through these stages, we can then set about purging the narc from our heart, mind, and life.

Only by progressing through the stages that I'm going to outline can you truly move from the feeling of being trapped in the relationship to the feeling that you can live without your abuser; you know you deserve better, but passing through these five stages allows you to put action to that knowledge.

Escaping the narcissist stage one: being aware of the abuse

As you're reading this particular book, I'm guessing that you're at this stage already (at least). You're aware that you're being mistreated, disrespected and abused, and you've matched your partner's behaviors with those typically shown from a malignant narcissist. Being aware that you're being abused at the hands of a dangerous abuser is your first part of the journey to freedom.

Becoming aware that what you're enduring is actually *abuse* often happens after the initial phase of the relationship where you've been lovebombed and idealized by the narc - once they begin showing you flickers of who they truly are, you may even brush it off to begin with. But, their emotional torture doesn't seem to relent, even if they promise you otherwise.

You will look back at the beginning of the relationship with your abuser, and often you'll reminisce how things were perfect and how happy you were. Of course, at that time you were in a place of blissful unawareness - you didn't imagine what the narc had in store for you. You entered the relationship with good, honest intentions, and (as you should), you expected the same in return.

Invariably, something alarming happens that disrupts your view of your other half, or a series of unsettling incidents occurs to trigger your awareness that your spouse may not be all they promised you. Even then, when you first discovered that something was amiss with your partner, you probably didn't call it abuse; much less would you have pinned it to something as specific as malignant narcissism.

Regardless, at this stage, you become all too aware that someone who says they love you shouldn't want to do the horrifying things that you've had to endure.

With these events being the first glimpses we get of what's behind the mask, it's common to brush these aside as being 'one-off's', or blame external circumstances such as the abuser being stressed at work. It's often at this time, with the helping hands of the narcissist, that we begin to blame ourselves for the horrible treatment the narc subjects us to. *If they weren't like this at the beginning of the relationship, then it must be you who brings out this nasty streak in them... right?*

As you're already at this stage at the minimum (because you're here reading this book), then you may already be at the next stage:

Escaping the narcissist stage two: understanding that the behavior is abusive.

Getting to this second stage means coming to accept what's happening - that it's in fact abuse is taking place. You can no longer brush it off or cast it to the back of your mind. There have been too many horrific, nasty incidents for you to not accept this behavior for what it is. The beginning stage of idealization starts to fade away, and we get so disheartened, miserable, and confused that we start to seek answers: *why am I being treated this way?* By this point, you've already blamed yourself so much that it's hard to look outside of that perspective - but, because you try so hard to appease and please your abuser, you begin to realize that perhaps it isn't you that makes them behave the way they do. You start to search for other explanations.

This may be by talking to other people who've experienced something similar to you, or even just listening to others explain what an abusive relationship means. It could even be that, like me and so many others, you turned to the internet, books, and blogs to help you work out what you're going through and why. You may have read up on narcissism and a lightbulb went off in your head: *finally, you have a name to put to the way you've been mistreated.*

The flipside to this is having to digest the sheer magnitude of what we have in front of us: a malignant narcissist. The discovery of this can be bittersweet because we can stop blaming ourselves for the abuse, but, we've uncovered just how fierce and unrelenting what we're up against is.

It's at this point that we realize that we now have two conflicting realities: one that the narcissist offers us, and another one that we find from outside of the relationship. The latter of these gives us a new and logical understanding of the narcs behavior. As time goes on, as we keep on trudging through this stage, we begin to consistently see a discrepancy between the narcissist's words and their vile deeds.

At this point, our newfound understanding contributes to the cognitive dissonance that slowly seeps into our feelings. We can no longer keep using denial and 'burying our heads in the sand' in order to cope. During stage two, we have new (more logical) information that competes with the narcissist's words or their version of events.

Escaping the narcissist stage three: coming to accept their behavior as destructive

Looking back, I now realize that I remained at stage two for quite some time. I was utterly confused, heartbroken, and, instead of using my newfound knowledge about narcissism to free myself from my abuser, I tried to find other ways to deal with the abuse instead. This only held me back from recovery and breaking free emotionally from my abuser.

I so desperately wanted the relationship to work; I didn't want it to have been a waste of my time or a fruitless endeavor, especially after I'd been put through so much by him. I wanted to think that I'd be rewarded with this love in the end - that by putting up with his abuse for so long, I'd of 'passed his test' and he would finally love me like he ought to have loved me all along.

Eventually, stage three is something you come face-to-face with. For a long time, I ignored it, and refused to acknowledge its presence. Sadly, it's often only time that can bring us to stage three - there's no accelerator, I'm afraid. It's only after we've endured so much toxicity and abuse that we finally accept that our abuser is destroying us. This acceptance comes after a lot of persistent vile treatment from the narc, coupled with the lack of anything ever changing or getting better.

By stage three, the idealization phase is normally so far in the past that we don't see many (if any) glimpses of it at all anymore. Combine this with the fact that we've been subjected to so much hurt, pain, heartache, and betrayal, we no longer feel as if we're the person we were when we first got into the relationship. Add onto this that we've been conditioned throughout the relationship not to talk about the abuse or discuss our feelings about what we've had to endure, we feel utterly defeated and now have nowhere to turn but the truth: that the relationship is bad for us. Not only that, but we are better off out of the relationship than in it. This can be a heartbreaking discovery and one that we can toy with many times before we finally accept it.

And yet, even after we accept this as truth, it's still incredibly hard to remove yourself from the narcissist. No matter how many times we've been lied to and let down, we find ourselves being drawn back in again and again and again.

This, without a doubt, causes additional suffering: knowing what is happening but still feeling incapable of escaping. Now not only does your abuser's behaviors not match their words, but you also have to deal with the painful truth that no longer does yours, either.

We end up almost emotionally paralyzed when our two versions of reality are competing, especially when one of those realities is created by the narcissist. It's at this point that we often begin to develop a sense of learned helplessness. This is in direct response to not being able to get what we want effectively, either one way or another from the relationship. We're unable to either to leave our abuser or be treated in the way we know we deserve - we feel utterly powerless.

At one of the lowest points in my relationship with my narcissistic ex, I recall feeling that the only way I would escape the relationship is in a casket. I'm so thankful that I was wrong.

Escaping the narcissist stage four: finding the lost and broken pieces of you and reassembling them

The learned helplessness we develop over time is, of course, an illusion. It's yet another one of the narcs manipulative tactics they utilize to retain you and your narcissistic supply.

Overcoming these abusive and manipulative tactics that are used to keep us helpless is the next stage that we enter before we're able to take the action of leaving the narcissistic relationship.

The gaslighting, the lies, the blame, the deceit, and the cruelness that the narc uses to keep us under their control are now things we're aware of - we know the narcissist for what they are now. However, we feel fear and dread about the prospect of leaving our abuser because of the unknown future and not knowing what life will be like without be the relationship we've given so much of ourselves to.

Despite now knowing them for what they are, we still feel guilt at the thought of doing anything to harm or upset the narcissist. It's as if we're betraying them, and this then makes us begin thinking of the good times we had with them. At times it feels as if we shouldn't give up on them, no matter how horribly they've treated us.

There's an overwhelming sadness when you think about leaving the narcissist. After all, it's a loss of a huge presence in your life, and to rid yourself of that is hard, no matter how poorly you've been treated by them - there's no doubt you care about them and yearn for the outcome you wish the relationship had. You dread the rage you'll encounter when you leave the narcissist, and the idea of that is enough to put you off leaving them - you feel like it's easier to deal with their abuse than it is to put yourself through their dramatic, vengeful response to you leaving them.

However, despite feeling all of those things, you can overcome them by understanding that they're manufactured by the narcissist and the things they've done to you. They are merely manipulative tactics; all part of the narcissist's illusion to keep you under their toxic spell.

The real hurt at this point, from my experience, is trying to come to terms with the knowledge that a narcissist won't change, and no matter how much you plead with them, they'll never be faithful and honest. The real feeling is the constant state of fight or flight mode we find ourselves in. The lies and the gaslighting cause us to feel a real sense of unease and harbor obsessive thoughts. We constantly have that persistent feeling where we can't relax into or feel safe.

Step four is about letting those emotions and fears guide us ad of battling them and trying to bury them, it's about facing them. By doing this, however painful it is to face, we can begin to rebuild our strength. Stage four is about facing the truth; the *real* truth, not the narcissist's truth.

Overcoming the toxic tactics of the narcissist means the following:

Recognizing what they're doing and what their agenda is when they try to manipulate you.

No longer treating the bad behavior you have been subjected to throughout the relationship as acceptable, just in order to avoid an argument.

Not letting their lies and manipulation sway your behavior, thoughts or actions in their favor (i.e, choosing to believe that they're correct when they gaslight you, and doubting your own instinct and perceptions.)

Beginning to see yourself as empowered, and completely undeserving of the treatment you've been exposed to. During times when you feel emotionally drained and battered, it may be a case of faking it until you make it.

Stage four is an enlightened one. You feel a flurry of different emotions, but through them all, you begin to find your sense of self again. You have spurts of empowerment. You sometimes feel like you're rising from your subdued shell and are ready to tackle the goliath that is the malignant narcissist. Yet, it can be extremely difficult because nothing brings on those emotions other than the conscious effort on your part to push back against the abuse in a meaningful way. It's so simple yet so hard at the same time, but it's entirely doable. More than that, it's a necessity.

On top of this, you can use the malignant narcissist's treatment of you against them in your journey to detaching from them.

For example:

Use silent treatment as a time to clear your head. Don't sit and overthink about them or what you've 'done' to them - without the narcs stifling influence to suppress you during an episode of silent treatment, you can begin to think more clearly about your situation and about what's been going on in the relationship. You can think more about you, and how you're feeling and think about things that make you happy. You can use this tactic that the narcissist uses against them; the silent treatment is designed to work you up, get you anxious, uneasy and make you feel guilty. Push back on this by not feeling like that; make a conscious effort to use this time wisely for yourself. You're away from the immediate influence and emotional disruption from the narc, so take that time and indulge in your own thoughts. The narc certainly won't be banking on you doing that.

There will be no direct gaslighting during silent treatment, so you can start having some empowering thoughts, dream about your goals and envision a more peaceful, happy life.

Escaping the narcissist stage five: shifting your mindset to take action

Stage four sees you change the psychological attitude you have towards yourself and consider your ability to do something about the toxic situation you're in.

In this stage, it's about mindset changes in how we view the narcissist. We've readied ourselves to face the truth and know what kind of relationship we're in. This has built a steady foundation to take action and remove yourself from the toxic situation physically and mentally.

This is where true recovery really begins because we now have more control over our own actions, regardless of the fear, sadness, and guilt we feel at how it will affect the narcissist.

Best practice is as follows. Even if you're not ready to follow through with these yet, it's good to know what you're preparing yourself for in the future:

Be prepared to go no-contact with the narcissist forever

Refrain from idealizing the narcissist post-split

It's two steps. It seems so easy, and I know it's not. But, it's a requirement if you're ever going to be free and heal. Depending on what stage you're at, you may be thinking to yourself, '*I can fix my relationship - I don't need to leave. I'll fix it before it comes to that,*' or you may even be at that stage where you're ready to take action. I know it sounds very black and white, and I know it's much more complex than those two sentences above.

Stage five is an angst-ridden volcano erupting, a panicked freefall into a future that you never had planned. It's a blind spot, an emotional roller coaster. It's the death of a relationship, the mourning of the person you never really had, fraught with uncertainty.

However, stage five is also the point of no return, where we have that major psychological shift towards the narcissist. We no longer see the relationship as simply being bad for us, and we truly begin to see the narc as a dangerous person who we not only *know* we need to be away from, we actually *want* to be away from them.

Stage five means we've finally chosen ourselves. We're no longer willing to accept the treatment and toxic behavior from the narc. We'd rather venture into the scary unknown that endure the living nightmare that is the malignant narcissist.

We choose to rebuild and recover.

***

One of the worst things that can happen to you has happened - you were, or are, involved with a malignant narcissist. This may sound extreme to say it's 'one of the worst' things that can happen, but let me put this in perspective for you.

When considering your happiness, health and your mental state, the worst thing that can happen for you is to live with an angry, resentful, cruel and sadistic partner. This, in turn, depletes your of your health and happiness and strips you of the values you once held so dear. This, unbeknownst to you, creates your identity as a victim.

'Victim' is a word I winced at for a long time. When I was referred to as a 'victim' by others, including my therapist, I would recoil in disgust at the word - and at myself. I didn't want to be labeled as something that made me feel so weak, ashamed and fragile. Over time, however, I learned to embrace the word for what it was: a way to describe the person I became because of somebody else's vile behavior towards me. I had nothing to be ashamed of. The shame ought to lay with the abuser, not the victim. If you remember little else from this book, I want you to remember that.

I hope this book has given you a better understanding of malignant narcissism and has helped you in knowing that there are others - just like you - who have endured the same heartache, pain and torture. I also hope this book has gone some way in giving you hope that you can overcome the effects of a toxic narcissist, and can find comfort in knowing that I and so many others have recovered, thrived and blossomed after such a sadistic and disturbing relationship.

As always, do let us know if this has been beneficial for you. You can leave a review, and if you'd like to offer up a little of your own story with it, that would be unbelievably valuable to someone who reads it who's in an abusive relationship. You can also find us on Instagram @escapethenarcs - we reply to all DM's, so please feel free to get in touch. We welcome all into our community of survivors and thrivers, and we're currently building up escapethenarcissist.com to become a site for all of us to share our experiences. Check it out, and if you would like, you can let us know your story. If not, you can use the site as a resource to understand narcissism and find inspiration from those who have fought its toxicity and won.

Here's to healing.

About the Publisher

Escape The Narcissist is about helping you find your self-worth, offering you some thought provoking ideas to change your life and aiding you in revitalizing your relationships.

With that in mind, Escape The Narcissist has one core relationship we want to focus on: the one you have with yourself.

Our website was born from a place of darkness. We've all, at some point in our lives, been on the receiving end of ill treatment from others. From being a victim of a narcissistic relationship to being mistreated by those who should protect us and not being shown the respect we deserve, these toxic relationships can affect us more than we realise.

Whilst the people behind the content of our site and books all have their own ideas and stories, they have one thing in common: they've all overcome toxicity in their lives and want to share their story.

The content of the stories, pieces of advice and actionable life changes within this site all aim to inspire, provoke a healthier way of thinking, and help to heal any negative effects you've been left with at the hands of other people.

escapethenarcissist.com

Lightning Source UK Ltd.
Milton Keynes UK
UKHW011434200921
390901UK00003B/983